HOLIDAYS ★ HOLIDAYS

AMERICANS ALL

SEVENTH PRINTING

Printed in the United States of America by
the Polygraphic Company of America, Inc.

Library of Congress Catalog Card Number:
55-5405

THE FIRST BOOK OF
HOLIDAYS

by BERNICE BURNETT

Pictures by
MARJORIE GLAUBACH

FRANKLIN WATTS, INC.
NEW YORK, N. Y.

All kinds of holidays

Sometimes when you wake up in the morning — even before you open your eyes to see if it is sunny or rainy — you know that the day is special. "Something is going to happen today," you say, "something wonderful! Today's a holiday!" And you can't help feeling excited and happy.

Most holidays are days which are set aside for rest or play to help remember something important that happened or to honor some great person. Other holidays are days which used to have real meaning in our lives but which have almost been forgotten. Often we still celebrate the traditions which are connected with them.

1

Many of our most important holidays are **religious holidays**. The holiday that Americans observe most often is a religious one, the Sabbath. It is a holy day that is set aside as a day of worship and rest. (The word "holiday" once was "holy day.") Christians keep the Sabbath on Sunday, and Jews celebrate it on Saturday.

Another kind of holiday are **national holidays**. These are days that the people in a whole country want to remember. The birthday of the United States is celebrated by all Americans on Independence Day, July 4, each year. And we observe as a nation a day of thanksgiving.

Some holidays are **legal holidays** — that is, holidays our states set apart by law. On these holidays all ordinary business stops. There is no national legal holiday enacted by the Congress of the United States, but in all the states New Year's Day, Independence Day, Labor Day, and Christmas are legal holidays.

The President of the United States or the governors of any of the states may declare a holiday on a certain day of a certain year by making an announcement or proclamation. These are called **holidays by proclamation**. The fourth Thursday in November each year is proclaimed by the President and state governors as Thanksgiving Day.

Regional holidays are days that are celebrated in a particular part of the country. In Maine and Massachusetts, for instance, April 19 is a holiday — Patriots' Day. The Revolutionary War patriots are especially honored in these two New England states.

2

Everyone celebrates in the way he likes best his own personal holiday — his birthday. He may have a party, a cookout, or just do whatever he chooses to that day. Usually he will have a birthday cake decorated with icing and a candle for each year of his life, plus one "to grow." And most families make a very special holiday of the parents' and grandparents' wedding anniversaries. Sometimes, to celebrate the occasion, they have dinner out, and other times they have a party and serve their favorite dishes. Or someone may decide to give them a surprise party. This is often nicest of all! **Family holidays** such as birthdays and anniversaries are very important in our lives.

New Year's Day

An old Roman god with two faces — one for looking forward to the new year and the other for looking back at the old — may seem to have nothing at all to do with Americans today. But we follow the custom of staying up late on December 31 to watch the old year out and the New Year in because of Janus, the Roman god of beginnings and endings and openings and closings.

It was Julius Caesar, the Roman emperor, who decided that the year should start in the month he named January in honor of Janus, the god of beginnings. Before Caesar's time Romans celebrated the New Year when spring came. But the men who studied the stars and the sun to work out Caesar's calendar made the year too long. In 1582 Pope Gregory III changed the calendar to the one we use today. In the change New Year's Day was moved from January 14, Janus' festival day, to January 1.

The New Year's Eve customs of making noise — blowing horns or whistles and ringing bells — and wearing costumes or silly hats probably go back to the Roman midwinter festival.

New Year's Day itself is a legal holiday all over the United States. Since it is a day of beginnings, many people like to begin new programs or stop old habits. They may make "New Year's resolutions." They say, *"This* year I won't start any arguments with anyone."

Or, "I'm going to save some money every week."

And they like to have parties and exchange good wishes for the coming year with their friends.

Some of the things people used to do on New Year's Day are now almost forgotten. Once kings and emperors grew rich on the gifts their subjects presented to them on each New Year. There aren't many kings or emperors any more and no one sends costly gifts on New Year's Day to those who are left. But way back in Roman days friends gave each other presents on that day. In France and other European countries, people still exchange gifts on New Year's Day.

Only the terms "pin money" and "start with a clean slate" are left to remind us of two customs from old England. Husbands used to give their wives "pin money" on New Year's Day to buy enough pins for the coming year. Pins were made by hand out of wire and they were very expensive. After machines were developed to make pins cheaply "pin money" for pins disappeared.

5

Careful housewives in England never let a New Year's Day pass without calling in a chimney sweep to clean the soot from the chimneys and the slates of the roof. They believed it would bring good luck for the household to "start with a clean slate."

Lincoln's Birthday

The birthday of Abraham Lincoln on February 12 is celebrated as a legal holiday in the northern and western states. It is not observed in the southern states.

Lincoln was the sixteenth president of the United States. During his term in office the only war which ever divided our country — the Civil War, or the War Between the States — was fought. The war lasted for four years, from 1861 to 1865. Although some of the southern states had wanted to leave the United States and form a country of their own, the Union was preserved under the leadership of President Abraham Lincoln.

Lincoln has been called the "Great Emancipator" because he issued the famous Emancipation Proclamation which freed the slaves who had been held in the rebellious states. Later, in 1865, Congress passed the Thirteenth Amendment to the Constitution, which freed all the slaves.

Many of the southern states pay tribute to the memory of Robert E. Lee, commander of the Confederate armies during the Civil War, on January 19, which is a legal holiday in twelve states, and to the memory of Jefferson Davis, president of the Confederacy, on June 3.

7

St. Valentine's Day

Everybody knows that Valentine's Day is a special day for sweethearts, but nobody knows exactly why people first came to celebrate it. And over the years, many different stories have grown up about how this very old holiday came to be.

One of the loveliest tales goes back to Roman times but comes to us from England. According to this legend, the birds choose their mates on February 14, for they know that spring is not far away. Young people follow the example of the birds, and choose their sweethearts too on St. Valentine's Day.

Other stories about St. Valentine's Day say that it is celebrated in memory of two Roman martyrs named Valentine who lived long ago. When the Romans became Christian the Church made them stop celebrating a rough and noisy festival, called the Lupercalia, which fell on February 15. St. Valentine's Day, in honor of the two Valentines, took its place and was observed a day earlier.

But one of the customs of the Lupercalia was kept, and it may be the origin of our valentines of today. On the day the Lupercalia was held the Romans put the names of young men and women into a box and then drew them out, two by two. The man and woman whose names were drawn at the same time were expected to be sweethearts for the next year. They often sent each other gifts and sweet messages.

Much later these messages were sent by mail and came to be called "valentines." Today children often carry dozens of pretty paper valentines to school and stuff them into cardboard valentine boxes for their friends. Sometimes the valentines are not pretty at all, but are funny instead. Of course young people who really *are* sweethearts may send valentine cards, gifts of flowers, or heart-shaped boxes of candy. Because though children have fun on St. Valentine's Day, it really is a day for sweethearts.

St. Valentine's Day is not a legal holiday in any of the states, but is a traditional one.

Washington's Birthday

We celebrate the birthday of George Washington, the first president of the United States, on February 22. When the thirteen colonies made their Declaration of Independence from Great Britain in 1776, the American Revolution started. The American colonists were dissatisfied with English rule, and believed that it was right for this country to be free. George Washington served as Commander-in-Chief of the first American army. After the Revolution was won, his fellow-countrymen honored Washington for his great leadership by electing him president.

During Washington's lifetime, and ever since his death, our country has celebrated the anniversary of his birth. Washington's Birthday is a legal holiday in all the states except in Idaho. Before that day each year American schools honor the great man who has been called "first in peace and first in war and first in the hearts of his countrymen." Parties are often held, and people have cherry pie and log-shaped cakes decorated with chocolate icing and cherries to celebrate the event. But the famous story about George Washington chopping down the cherry tree, which these symbolize, is not true!

St. Patrick's Day

No one is surprised any more that one of our holidays is in honor of the patron saint of another country, for we have been celebrating it for so long. This holiday honors St. Patrick, the patron saint of Ireland. Americans of Irish descent and of many other national origins celebrate St. Patrick's Day on March 17. They march in parades, gather together for big dinners, dance Irish jigs, and sing Irish songs.

A huge St. Patrick's Day parade is held in New York City. Other cities, too, hold St. Patrick's Day parades. One of the largest and oldest is in Boston. Everyone wears something green in memory of Ireland, the Emerald Isle. Some wear shamrocks, little three-leaved clovers. And everywhere along the way of the parade Irish flags fly and people sing and whistle the Irish tunes that the bands play.

The love and reverence that the Irish people feel for their patron saint is shown in the old saying: "St. Patrick found Ireland all heathen and left it all Christian."

St. Patrick was born in Scotland in about the year 387. Pirates captured him when he was sixteen years old and took

11

him to Ireland, where the people worshiped idols. He was sold as a slave, and escaped after six years. He went to Europe to study religion and to become a priest and a bishop, and returned to Ireland to teach the people about the God he believed in. Although he was captured by the Irish enemies of his faith twelve times, he always escaped and went on teaching. We celebrate the anniversary of his death in 493 as St. Patrick's Day.

There are many wonderful stories about St. Patrick, and the most famous is that he drove the snakes out of Ireland. This is only a legend, but the Irish will tell you that you can't find a snake in the whole of Ireland!

Easter

If ever there is a day when the sun dances in the sky for joy, that day must be Easter! There is an old folk belief that this is exactly what happens at dawn on Easter Sunday.

For Christians Easter is a day of great gladness, since it celebrates the time when Jesus Christ rose from the dead. The Christian churches teach that because of this all people who believe in Christ will have everlasting life.

Easter is one of the greatest religious festivals of the year. For a long time, during the early days of the Christian church, it was celebrated on different dates. But in the year 325 a council of churchmen met at a town called Nicea and fixed the date for Easter as the first Sunday following the first full moon after March 21.

In many churches the celebration begins about forty days before Easter Sunday, on Ash Wednesday. This period is called Lent, an old word meaning spring. Lent is celebrated in memory of the forty days that Jesus spent praying alone in the wilderness before He went out to teach and help people. During Lent many people make sacrifices such as giving up some of the things they like to do, or not eating certain foods they enjoy.

The Sunday before Easter is called Palm Sunday, in memory of a journey Jesus made into the city of Jerusalem. People along the way covered the path before him with palm branches, and many churches today commemorate this on Palm Sunday by giving palm branches to those in church.

In the week before Easter are two very important holidays —

Holy Thursday and Good Friday. Holy Thursday is celebrated in memory of Christ's last supper with his disciples. Good Friday is a sad day. It marks the time when Christ died on the cross on the hill at Calvary. Church altars are left bare, and candles are unlighted. Only solemn music is played. Sometimes churches are draped with black cloth.

On Easter Sunday the Lenten period of sorrow and fasting ends. Church altars are decorated with beautiful Easter lilies. Candles are lighted with new fire. Church services celebrate the day that Christ rose from the dead. Sometimes all the members of a church go high on a hill to hold sunrise services on Easter morning. Large crosses marking these places can be seen against the sky for many miles.

Although Easter is a religious holiday, we still follow customs that go back to an ancient festival that was held at this time of year long before Christianity. At this season the ancient Anglo-Saxon people used to have a festival in honor of Eostre, their goddess of light and spring. And her name has come down as the English name of the Christian holiday.

One of the old customs that have come from early times is coloring Easter eggs. Colored eggs were used in the spring celebrations of the ancient Persians, Egyptians, Greeks, and Romans. You may think that the celebration of the belief in everlasting life is very far indeed from celebrating Easter with prettily decorated eggs. But it is not so strange as it seems, for the egg holds within itself the beginning of new life.

There used to be an old belief that on Easter Sunday a rabbit lays bright red and blue and yellow and purple eggs in the new grass. Often today, in the days before Easter, parents and children spend time decorating eggs with gay designs. Late on Saturday night they steal out and hide the eggs. The next morning the children get up early to hunt for them. Afterwards they sometimes have an egg roll on a lawn. The Easter egg roll on the White House lawn in Washington is famous.

Easter eggs have been used to look at, to play with, and to eat for a long time. Artificial eggs are made out of painted wood, glass, china, or spun sugar. In old Russia especially beautiful ones were given as gifts at Easter. Some were so lovely and made of such expensive materials decorated with jewels that they have been kept as treasures. Those that were made of sugar had little scenes inside that could be seen through a transparent place at one end.

Putting on new clothes at Easter is a very old custom. Early Christians were baptized on Easter Sunday and wore new white garments for the week that followed as a sign of their new innocence of soul. Today most people enjoy taking off their heavy winter clothes and starting to wear the fresh light clothes of spring. And they like to see the "Easter parade" of gaily dressed people strolling home from church.

April Fool's Day

If anyone were to wish you a Happy New Year on April 1 you would be sure he was playing an April Fool joke. But April Fool's Day started in France, some scholars believe, just because April 1 once *was* New Year's Day. In 1564 the King of France adopted the calendar that is used today, and the new year began on January 1. Many people forgot or didn't like the new date. They were called "April fools."

Frenchmen used to exchange gifts with their friends on April 1 when that date began the year. They kept the custom of sending gifts on that date. But after the change in the calendar the kinds of gifts changed too. People started to send silly or worthless gifts, or packages made to look like something they were not.

That is one explanation for this holiday. But another explanation may be that this light-hearted festival is in honor of the return of spring. There is a good reason for believing that this is so, for there have been other just such foolish celebrations in the spring.

An ancient Roman festival in honor of Ceres, the goddess of grain, was held at the beginning of April. An old holiday called Holi filled with joke-making and fun is celebrated in India in early April. On the night before Holi the people all over India light huge bonfires. Then they begin to beat great drums, louder and louder. On the day itself boys and girls blow bright powders or colored liquids over the people in the streets. Before long everyone's clothes are bright green or red or purple or all colors mixed together. People dance and sing and eat sweets all day long. Everyone loves Holi!

Pan American Day

Our own country and twenty other American republics observe Pan American Day each year on April 14. Pan American Day is the anniversary of the creation in 1890 of the Pan American Union, made up of the republics of South, Central, and North America.

Some of the American countries began holding conferences as early as 1826 with the aim of forming friendly relations with one another. The First International Conference of American States, which included all the independent nations in this hemisphere, was held in Washington, D. C., in 1889.

We have celebrated Pan American Day since 1931. There are ceremonies in the Pan American Building in Washington, and the flags of all the Pan American nations fly there. Schools and interested groups present programs showing the ways in which the Pan American countries are working together to help each other.

Arbor Day

The first Arbor Day was started by a man named J. Sterling Morton in 1872. He noticed the soil of the treeless plains of Nebraska, where he lived, getting dryer and blowing away. He made up his mind to do everything he could to restore the earth's richness. The best way to do this, he believed, was to plant trees. After much talking he convinced the people of Nebraska that a tree-planting day should be established.

More than a million trees were planted in Nebraska the first year, and it became known as the Tree Planters' State. Mr. Morton is called the Father of Arbor Day. Nebraska celebrates Arbor Day each year on his birthday, April 22.

Other states soon followed Nebraska's example, and now every state in the Union celebrates this day on various dates. Most observe it in April. Where there is not a fixed date, the governors of the states proclaim a certain day as Arbor Day.

Most schools have special tree-planting ceremonies to mark

the day. Sometimes children name the trees they plant for a famous author or statesman. In certain places there are groves of trees, now full grown, that were named and planted by school children long ago.

Many countries have days similar to our Arbor Day, and there have been tree-planting days in ancient times. When a child was born to a family of Aztec Indians the parents planted a tree, and so did the Jews in ancient Palestine. Nowadays the children in Israel plant trees on the festival of the New Year of the trees. From our own and other countries Jewish children and their parents send money to plant trees in Israel.

May Day

Holiday traditions change. New holidays are born and old ones die out. May Day is one of the holidays that have almost disappeared. Nowadays labor unions hold parades on May Day as well as on Labor Day, but once kings and queens, ordinary grownups and children in Europe and in our own country, celebrated May Day. Today very little is left to remind us of what May Day used to be like.

23

Scholars who study ancient customs believe that May Day customs go back to an old Roman holiday celebrating the blossoming of flowers. In some places in our own country people still deliver May baskets. Children visit their friends' houses early in the morning or at twilight, without being seen, and leave fancy little baskets filled with pretty spring flowers on the doorsteps. In Rome people used to make similar offerings of flowers to statues of Flora, the goddess of flowers.

Certain schools still celebrate May Day. Some choose an especially pretty girl to be Queen of the May and rule over the festival. They wind a long pole, called a maypole, with ribbons, and decorate it with flowers. Then they stand it upright on the lawn and dance about it, weaving in and out with ribbons that hang from its top, until it is striped with colored ribbons. Sometimes they roll hoops across the lawn and try to see whose hoop can keep rolling longest.

In England during the rule of Queen Elizabeth I people went into the forest at dawn on May Day to bring back flowers and branches of trees. They would set up a maypole in the town square and decorate it with ribbons and flowers. But in 1660, when a group of colonists at Merrymount, Massachusetts, started the custom in this country, the Puritan settlers were furious, since they frowned on any kind of fun or gaiety. They hacked the pole to pieces. And in order to remind everyone to be serious instead of gay, they changed the name of the settlement from Merrymount to Mount Dagon, after an idol that was destroyed in Biblical times.

Mother's Day

A special day for mothers is rather a new holiday in our country. In 1915 Congress asked the President of the United States to proclaim Mother's Day as a day to be remembered throughout the nation. After this presidents have issued such a proclamation each year.

Miss Anna Jarvis of Philadelphia is known as the founder of Mother's Day, for she spent her life trying to make sure that one day a year would be set aside to honor mothers. It was Miss Jarvis who started the custom of wearing a flower on Mother's Day. And now most people wear a red rose or a pink carnation on that day if their mother is living or a white flower if she is dead.

There are days to honor mothers in other countries, and holidays celebrating motherhood date back to very ancient times.

In India there is a ten-day long festival called Durga Puja in honor of Durga, the Divine Mother. She is the mother of the goddess of the arts and the goddess of beauty and wealth and of the god of wisdom and the god of war. During her festival people bring offerings of flowers or fruits and vegetables or animals to the temples. And children honor their own mothers as part of the celebration for the Divine Mother, and take gifts or greetings to them.

A holiday called "Mothering Sunday" comes about midway through Lent in England. Then grownups visit their mothers and take gifts to them, and small children give their mothers presents they have made themselves.

Memorial Day

Memorial Day, May 30, is a holiday that isn't a celebration. It is the saddest of all days for our country, for it is in memory of the hundreds of thousands of our men who have been killed in war.

This day used to be called Decoration Day, and sometimes it still is so called. It is the day when families and friends decorate the graves of soldiers with flags and wreaths of flowers.

Memorial Day began to be observed soon after the Civil War, or War Between the States, ended. The war that divided our country was terrible and bitter. And although today the North and South both are proud that our nation is united, Memorial Day still is held on different dates in the two parts of the country.

In the North the holiday comes on May 30. The South observes Confederate Memorial Day in memory of the soldiers who fought in the Confederate Army. In Mississippi, Florida, Georgia, and Alabama the day falls on April 26; in North and South Carolina, on May 10; in Virginia, on May 30; and in Kentucky, Louisiana, and Tennessee, on June 3. Some southern cities observe the day on still other dates.

Father's Day

Fathers have their own special holiday every year on the third Sunday in June. In order to show them how much they are loved all year round, on that day their children and grandchildren write them notes, send them greeting cards, and give them presents.

Father's Day is not an official holiday, and it has not been widely celebrated for very long. The idea of having such a holiday is believed to have started with Mrs. John Bruce Dodd of Spokane, Washington, who wanted to honor her own father. The first public celebration of Father's Day took place in Spokane on the third Sunday in June, 1910. Everyone who went to church was asked to wear a red rose if his father were living, or a white one if he were dead. Other celebrations were held from time to time in various places all over the country, and now the day is celebrated each year.

Flag Day

Each year June 14 is set aside as a day to honor our flag. On that day the red, white, and blue banner flies from all public buildings and from many homes and stores.

When the colonies had declared their independence from Great Britain they wanted a flag to be the symbol of the young nation. They chose a banner of thirteen stripes, seven red and six white stripes, with thirteen white stars on a blue field to represent the thirteen states. The stars were arranged in a circle. This was the first United States flag. Flag Day is the anniversary of the day it was adopted in 1777 by the Continental Congress.

But there have been many changes in the flag. When seven states had been added to the original thirteen, Congress passed an act which provided that a new star would be added to the flag for each new state, but the number of stripes would always be thirteen in honor of the thirteen original states.

For a long time there was no design for the position of the

stars, and flagmakers arranged them to suit themselves. But since 1912 the flag has been just as it is today — seven red and six white stripes, and forty-eight stars in six rows with eight stars in each row.

Children in almost every school in the country pledge their loyalty to the flag as a symbol of the country to which they belong:

I pledge allegiance to the flag of the United States of America and to the republic for which it stands; one nation under God, indivisible, with liberty and justice for all.

Independence Day

In the steeple of the State House of an eastern city a great bell rang out one day in 1776, summoning the people to meet in the town square.

Gradually the townspeople began to gather in the streets. Soon they were assembled in the State House yard where a man stood on a platform waiting to read a document to the crowd. The people grew solemn and silent while the paper was read.

The city was Philadelphia. The meeting place was what is now called Independence Square. The bell is the famous Liberty Bell. The document was the Declaration of Independence, which announced the American colonies' freedom from Great Britain.

The people of Philadelphia began then and there to celebrate

our country's independence. And all Americans, everywhere, have been celebrating it ever since on Independence Day, the Fourth of July. It is a legal holiday in every state of the Union.

At that first public reading of the Declaration of Independence long ago, there were great shouts of joy, for the people in the thirteen English colonies had been longing for their freedom. Men were already fighting against the tyrannies of the British king. Although the people knew that there would be more fighting and that perhaps many of them would lose their lives, they were strong in their belief that the colonies must free themselves from British rule.

Independence Day was not always celebrated on July 4. Indeed, that first celebration in Philadelphia did not take place until July 8, four days after the Declaration of Independence was signed. And since in those days there were no telephones or radios or television to carry the news over the country, the

story traveled slowly. It was two weeks before the news reached Williamsburg, Virginia — only 300 miles from Philadelphia — and the Declaration was officially announced there on July 25. But no matter just when the news reached them, the people in the colonies were proud and happy that they were part of a new nation.

In the early years of our country Independence Day was celebrated with parades and bonfires. Ships in the harbors were decorated with hundreds of flags. Cannons roared all day and into the night. Today jet planes streak across the skies while large cities hold parades and picnics, and speeches and firecrackers are often part of the celebration in smaller towns. In many places fireworks are not sold to individual buyers because they can be dangerous. But certain organizations are permitted to put on displays of fireworks to help show their happiness that our country is free and independent.

33

Labor Day

Most holidays are days of rest and play, and so is this one. But it celebrates just the opposite — work!

In 1882 a man named Peter J. McGuire first proposed a legal holiday for labor to be observed all over the United States. He was the president of the labor union called the United Brotherhood of Carpenters and Joiners of America. He suggested the first Monday in September as the date for the new holiday, and it was first observed in New York City on September 5, 1882. Five years later Oregon made the day a state holiday. Other states soon followed Oregon's example. Today the entire United States celebrates Labor Day as a legal holiday.

On this day people have a whole day to themselves for whatever they want to do. Sometimes they have the last picnic of the summer, for Labor Day comes at the beginning of fall, shortly before school starts. Sometimes workers march in parades and listen to speakers who tell how important labor is and talk about ways to make better living and working conditions. Everyone enjoys the Labor Day weekend, because it is the last weekend of the summer.

Columbus Day

Christopher Columbus, the explorer who opened the Western Hemisphere to settlers from Europe, was born in Genoa, Italy, in 1451. He became a sailor when he was young. Columbus didn't set out to find a new world, or even to prove that the world is round. He believed that by sailing west he could reach the east — the rich countries of China and Japan and India. But Columbus had no idea that our round earth is as big as it is, and he didn't know that the vast continents of North and South America lay to the west between Europe and Asia.

He tried to raise money to buy ships and supplies so that he could try to find a short route to the Indies, as all of the Orient was called. But people in Italy laughed at him, and the King of Portugal, whom he asked for help, would not listen to him.

At last Columbus went to King Ferdinand and Queen Isabella of Spain. They gave him money and ships and the men he needed to sail them. On August 3, 1492 he set out with three ships, the *Pinta,* the *Niña,* and the *Santa Maria.*

The ships sailed west for seventy-two days. When at last Columbus's ship, the *Pinta,* touched the shore of an island, Colum-

35

bus thought he had reached the Indies. He named the island San Salvador, but he called the people Indians. San Salvador is an island in the West Indies, to the southeast of Florida. Though it was not many years before people realized Columbus's mistake, the name Indians has never changed.

Columbus sailed to island after island in the West Indies. He returned to Spain and told the King and Queen of the wonders he had found. He made three other voyages of exploration and discovered such islands as Cuba, Haiti, and Jamaica. He even explored the coast of Venezuela, in South America.

Columbus was a man of vision and courage, but to the end of his days he never realized that instead of reaching the Indies, he had discovered an entire new world.

The first celebration to honor Columbus was held in New York City by a society called the Columbian Order. They erected the first public monument to Columbus on October 12, 1792. One hundred years later President Benjamin Harrison asked the people to celebrate Columbus Day on October 12 each year. In most states Columbus Day is now a legal holiday, and shortly before it schools have special programs based on Columbus's life.

United Nations Day

October 24, United Nations Day, is the anniversary of the day in 1945 when a union of nations from all over the world was formed in order to work for peace.

One of the ways in which members of the United Nations try to gain peace is by helping people in all parts of the world get enough food, good homes, good health, and education. They do a great many other things, too. They help settle arguments between countries. They have started an international fund to help children whose parents cannot take care of them properly. And they have acted together to help one country that was being attacked by another.

On United Nations Day many schools have special programs that tell about the work United Nations agencies do. The United Nations flag, a blue banner with a white wreath surrounding the world, flies from public buildings. Some churches hold special services. Men and women everywhere share the hope that the United Nations will help build a peaceful world.

37

Halloween

Of all the holidays we celebrate, Halloween, the evening of October 31, is perhaps the most fun. Yet this holiday used to be a fearsome one. Nowadays on Halloween we have parties and games and tricks, but once it was a time of terror and grief.

Halloween was first observed long before the birth of Christ by a people called the Celts, who lived in the British Isles and northern France. They feared that when winter came the sun they worshiped would be killed by the powers of darkness. They tried to save their god by paying a sort of tax to the forces of evil in a great ceremony on the night that we now know as Halloween. They burned some of their crops and animals in huge fires, hoping this would please the evil powers so that they would let the sun come back.

Of course modern people know that the sun always returns. Only a few weeks after Halloween, on December 21, the days begin to grow longer, and very slowly but very surely, the days begin to get warmer. The Celts, who did not know how the earth moves about the sun, thought this was because the powers of darkness had accepted their sacrifices on Halloween.

It is only in recent times that Halloween has become a holiday of fun. And even today there are traces of the customs that were a part of Halloween during the thousands of years in which it was a time of terror.

The black cat that decorates your Halloween parties is there because the Celts believed all the spirits of the dead were called together on the night of Halloween. A sort of court was held then by the Lord of Death who decided what form the spirits would take during the following year. Wicked spirits had to take the form of cats. Because of this people were afraid of cats. They believed cats had evil powers.

If you had dressed up as a witch on Halloween many years ago, it might have cost you your life! For although there never has been such a thing as a real witch, people believed in witches for a long time. And many innocent women were put to death simply because some people said they were witches.

All kinds of tales used to be told by persons who believed in witches. Some said that on Halloween certain women dressed in black clothes, took their brooms from their closets, and rode away on them to a secret meeting place. With them on their broomsticks rode their cats, the spirits of the dead. The witches would meet in groups of thirteen, and make magic spells to cause sickness or bad luck for their victims. They would work all night long stirring up a witches' brew and muttering curses.

Christians did everything they could to change these old beliefs about the evening of October 31. The Roman Catholic church set aside the first day of November to honor all the saints who had no special days of their own. This day became known as All Saints' or All Hallows' Day, and the night before it was called All Hallows' Even. This was shortened to Halloween. And after many hundreds of years, people stopped believing in witches and the powers of darkness.

For a long time there was still another belief in many countries about this mysterious night. It was the belief that between sunset and sunrise on Halloween the spirits of the dead were free to walk about the earth. When you wrap a sheet around yourself on Halloween and pretend to be a ghost, or dress in a costume that looks like a skeleton, with a skull for a mask, you probably resemble very closely the old idea of what these dead souls looked like.

The dead were very much in the thoughts of the living on Halloween. Families visited graves or churches to pray that the dead would rest in peace. And in England a very curious custom grew up. It was called "going a-souling." Men and women went about from house to house calling

> "A soul cake, a soul cake
> A penny or a soul cake!"

Housewives gave them little pastries called "soul cakes," and in return they said prayers for the souls of the dead.

Today most children dress up and go around on Halloween saying at each door

"Trick or treat!"

Almost everyone is ready with a treat of apples or cookies or a drink of cider. No one in this country today goes "a-souling," but the custom of begging on Halloween probably goes back to the old English one. To avoid being "tricked," storekeepers often join in Halloween fun by letting a group of youngsters decorate their store windows with gay drawings, and give prizes for the best work.

Jack-o'-lanterns became an American Halloween tradition only after many Irishmen immigrated to this country in the 1840's. It was an old Irish custom for children to hollow out a turnip, carve a grinning face on it, and put a lighted candle inside so they could use it as a lantern when going about on Halloween. But there are lots of pumpkins in this country, and they make even better jack-o'-lanterns than do turnips. Pumpkin jack-o'-lanterns are now a truly American part of this holiday.

Other Halloween customs come down from an ancient Roman fall festival. On the last day of October the Romans celebrated the gathering of the harvest fruits and worshiped Pomona, the goddess of the harvest. It is because of their custom of bringing apples and nuts as offerings to Pomona that on Halloween today you may bob for apples, throw an apple peel over your shoulder to find out the initial of your true love, or toss nuts into the fire to tell fortunes.

Veterans' Day

The newest holiday in the United States is Veterans' Day, proclaimed by President Eisenhower on June 1, 1954 as a day "to honor veterans on the eleventh of November of each year, a day of peace." Veterans' Day is observed by law in all the states.

From 1918 until 1954, this day was observed as Armistice Day in celebration of the Armistice that ended World War I. But because we have had the destruction and sorrow of war since then, it seemed more suitable to change the holiday to a day in honor of American veterans of all wars.

Today it is the custom to keep two minutes of silence at the hour when the fighting stopped in World War I. There are memorial services for the men who were killed in the wars in which the United States has fought. At the tomb of the Unknown Soldier in Washington, D. C., special services are held. An unknown American soldier who died in World War I lies buried there, and in honoring him we honor all of the brave men who fought for our country.

43

Election Day

A holiday that has a most serious purpose is Election Day. On that day every citizen in the United States who has reached the age of twenty-one has a chance to vote. Sometimes he chooses officers for his state or for the nation. Sometimes he decides on important issues. Sometimes he votes on amendments to our Constitution.

Voting in secret elections is a very great privilege. Only a few governments in all history have been run by the representatives of the people. Yet the United States has not always had "universal suffrage" — the right of every man and woman to vote. At times in our history men were not allowed to vote because they were slaves, or because they did not own property. But the Fourteenth and Fifteenth Amendments to the Constitution of the United States provided that no man should be kept from voting unless he had taken part in a rebellion or committed a crime.

Women were not allowed to vote in Federal elections for nearly one hundred and fifty years after our country was formed. Many women, and men, too, felt that women should have the same

voting rights as men. Some of them worked hard to try to get laws passed to give women the right to vote. Several states passed such laws, but it was not until the Nineteenth Amendment was adopted in 1920 that all of the women in the country at last could vote.

General Election Day, when Congressional elections are held, is set by Federal statute as the first Tuesday after the first Monday in November of every even-numbered year. The only exception is the state of Maine, which holds congressional elections on the second Monday in September. Every four years, on General Election Day, voters choose electors who in turn elect the President and Vice-President of the people's choice.

Every voter has a part in the election of the President, the Vice-President, and the Senators and Representatives from his state in Congress, our national legislature. In the separate states voters also elect their chief executives and members of the state legislatures. But local elections are not always held on General Election Day. Each state sets a date of its own choice for voting on matters of local interest.

45

Thanksgiving Day

On a day long ago the cool light of the early winter sun struck through the smoke from half a dozen fires in a clearing in the heavy forest. Each fire was watched over by two boys in knee breeches of deerhide. They took turns poking chips and logs into the fire and tugging at a rough forked branch that formed a spit, turning it so that the meat that hung there roasting would brown evenly. Nearby men were building tables of logs. Across the clearing smaller fires were burning beneath outdoor ovens. There the women and girls were busy, pushing great paddles loaded with pies of pumpkin and squash and mince into the ovens, and looking at their slowly browning crusts from time to time.

Some of the smallest children were going round and round in a circle in one corner. They wore little harnesses of buckskin

which were fastened to a large flat rock. As the children went round, the rock turned against another stone set in the earth beneath it. They were grinding yellow corn into coarse meal between the rocks.

Suddenly there was quiet. The children stopped turning the grinding stone. The women stood motionless. At the edge of the forest was a line of painted Indians.

The Indians came closer. In a moment shouts of welcome rang out. The settlers could see the Indians carrying wild turkeys and deer haunches slung across their shoulders. These were friendly Indians who had helped the settlers get used to this new country. They had come to share in the great feast that was being made ready.

These were the preparations for the first Thanksgiving in our land in the little colony at Plymouth, Massachusetts. The colonists had come to Massachusetts only the year before, and in the terrible cold of their first winter in New England almost half of their number died. Those who remained had planted their small store of corn, and they had reaped a good harvest. They had shot deer and wild turkey. They had made shelters from the coming cold, and a spirit of thanksgiving was in their hearts.

Governor William Bradford spoke for all of the little group when he set aside a time of Thanksgiving to God in the fall of 1621. For three days the colonists and their Indian guests sat together around the tables. They feasted and sang. They said prayers of thanksgiving. People took new courage for the hard work they had to do.

Nowadays each year the President of the United States proclaims a day of Thanksgiving on the fourth Thursday of November.

Many of the traditions of the Thanksgiving Day we celebrate as a legal holiday come from that first Thanksgiving celebration more than three hundred years ago. Wild turkeys that were hunted then in the forests of Plymouth were the great-great-great-great-grandfathers of the birds that appear on our holiday tables. Indian pudding — a sort of custard made with corn meal — is often served as a dessert. Squash and pumpkins like those our forefathers picked still go into pies for our traditional feast. The cranberries that grew wild in New England bogs are made into sauce. We decorate our tables with centerpieces of dried corn ears, grapes, pears, and other foods that are harvested in this season. Religious services of thanksgiving are held in churches throughout the country. For us, as for the early settlers in New England, the day is spent in eating the good things grown on our land and in giving thanks to God for the country we live in.

Christmas Day

Probably no story in all the world is told so often, in so many ways and in so many languages, as the story of the Nativity, the birth of Jesus Christ. When Jesus was born a new idea came into the world. It was the belief that God so loved the world that He gave His son, Jesus, to bring human beings eternal life.

This is the story of Christmas — the most beautiful holiday of all. It is truly a holy day; indeed, it is the holiest of days.

The English name Christmas is a shortening of Christ and Mass. In Latin the holiday is called Dies Natalis, the Birthday. Noël, the French name for this day, is taken from the Latin word "natalis."

Christmas is a wonderful time. At no other season is there so much excitement in the air! Some of the ways in which Christmas is observed in our country are very old, and some are quite new. Our houses are shining with lights and decorations hung with holly, ivy, evergreen boughs, and mistletoe. Before Christmas Day thousands and thousands of cards go from friends to friends all over the earth carrying "Best Wishes for a Merry Christmas."

Joyful Christmas music is everywhere. You can hear church bells pealing out "O Little Town of Bethlehem," "Joy to the World," or "Silent Night." And perhaps on Christmas Eve you join your friends and go from house to house singing carols.

If you do, you are following an old English custom. Long ago groups of singers called "Waits" used to wait outside windows to sing their Christmas songs. A hot drink and a coin or two were their reward. Some of the same music that rang out in the frosty air hundreds of years ago is sung by carolers today.

A familiar part of Christmas are scenes of the nativity, often called "crèches" (pronounced KRESH-ES), from the French word that means manger. Figures of Mary and Joseph and the baby Jesus in the manger, the animals of the stable, and the wise men bearing their gifts are lovingly arranged. Ever since the first

crèche was built by St. Francis of Assisi centuries ago many churches have had a crèche as part of their Christmas decorations. Today the windows of great stores often show the scene of the Nativity too.

When we look at the figures of the wise men, perhaps we can guess how one of our own Christmas customs began. For Christmas is the time of giving, and the first Christmas presents were the gifts of gold, frankincense, and myrrh that the wise men brought to the infant Jesus.

Their rich gifts weren't placed under a Christmas tree, as ours are, for that was long before there was such a thing as a Christmas tree.

The story of our modern Christmas tree lies deep in the past. The early German peoples feared and hated the freezing winters. They believed that evil spirits ran about in the dark days and long nights, trying to kill every living thing. Most of the plants and trees and bushes seemed to die, for their leaves dried and fell off, but the fragrant evergreens lived on. Men came to believe that wherever these bushes or trees were the life-snatching spirits could not go.

So they began to bring evergreens into their homes. They believed that the magic power of the evergreen would keep death from striking their families! Throughout the winter a tip

of a spruce or fir tree hung from the house rafters or was fastened upside down above the doorway. Sometimes the family decorated the branches with nuts and fruit. In later times they brought in entire trees and decorated them. Americans began to have gaily decorated Christmas trees in the nineteenth century.

Holly is one of the greens we use inside the house at Christmas. It may be because of its bright red berries and shiny green leaves that red and green have come to be Christmas colors.

When you hang a sprig of mistletoe at Christmas time, according to custom, you may kiss anyone who passes beneath it. For mistletoe has a very special meaning, and this is because of an old Scandinavian myth about Balder, the god of poetry.

Balder was protected from death by a magic power. Nothing that came from the earth or fire or water or air could harm him. But Loki, an evil spirit who was his enemy, made an arrow and tipped it with mistletoe. The ancients believed that this plant did not come from the earth or from fire or water or air. It grows on the oak tree, halfway between heaven and earth. The mistletoe dart struck and killed Balder, but his mother, Friga, wept until her love won out over death and brought the god back to life. Friga's tears became the pearl-like berries of the mistletoe. The mistletoe itself became a symbol of love, and so it is to this day.

When the mistletoe has been hung and the tree has been trimmed and the Christmas cards sent and the presents all wrapped, there still is more to do to get ready for this wonderful holiday. The special Christmas foods must be cooked — puddings and cookies and cakes. The rich fragrance of mince pies fills the air. Mince pies have been baked at Christmas time for hundreds of years. They represent the manger where Jesus was born and their spicy fruits stand for the gifts of the wise men.

To small children Christmas means just one thing: Santa Claus is coming! And although they never see him do this, they believe that on Christmas Eve Santa drives his sleigh drawn by eight prancing reindeer over the housetops. Wherever there are children he stops and comes down the chimney with a wonderful bag filled with toys. Each child hangs a stocking near the fireplace for Santa Claus to fill with oranges and nuts and little gifts. They are sure that Santa knows what they most want to have, and that he can find that very thing in his pack of toys.

The Santa Claus we know can be traced to an early Christian, St. Nicholas. He was the archbishop of Myra, an ancient town in Asia Minor. St. Nicholas was a kind and generous man who gave gifts to the poor and especially to children.

Stories about his gifts grew and grew. His fame spread to other countries. In Holland and Germany his name was changed from St. Nicholas to Santa Claus. The dark clothes of the bishop became the red fur-trimmed suit that Santa Claus wears.

The reason Santa Claus is supposed to come down the chim-

ney with his enormous pack goes back to an old belief in a legendary Scandinavian figure. The Norsemen, as the ancient Scandinavians are called, believed that a goddess named Hertha appeared in their fireplaces in the middle of winter to bring them good luck and happiness. Santa Claus, who brings gifts and toys, comes in the same way.

But the real meaning of Christmas is not giving presents. It is giving goodness and kindness and love. It is the blessing of the angel who told the shepherds of Christ's birth on the very first Christmas:

"On earth peace, good will toward men."

The Holydays of Obligation

Members of the Roman Catholic Church in the United States keep six special days called the Holydays of Obligation. On these days, as well as on all the Sundays of the year, Catholics are obliged to attend Mass. Special services are held in the churches.

The first of the holydays in the calendar year comes on January 1, the **Feast of the Circumcision** of Jesus Christ.

The second is **Ascension Day,** in memory of the day on which Christ ascended into heaven after He rose from the dead. It is celebrated forty days after Easter.

August 15 is **Assumption Day,** a holyday to celebrate the belief that the body of Mary, the mother of Jesus, was taken directly into heaven.

The **Feast of All Saints** on November 1 is set aside by the church to honor all of the saints who do not have a special feast day named for them.

The **Feast of the Immaculate Conception,** on December 8, celebrates the belief that Mary, the mother of Jesus, was conceived without original sin.

The birth of Jesus Christ is celebrated on December 25, a holyday known as the **Feast of the Nativity.**

Important Jewish Holidays

The Jewish New Year is called **Rosh Hashana**. It usually falls sometime in September. The Jews believe that on this day each year God examines a great Book of Life, in which there is a record of every act and every thought of all living persons.

Friends who meet on Rosh Hashana say to each other, "May you be inscribed for a good year." They mean that they wish what is written in the Book of Life will be good.

In the synagogue or temple, services open with a blast on the shofar, a trumpet made from a ram's horn. From Rosh Hashana until **Yom Kippur**, the Day of Atonement, ten days later, the people pray to God to forgive their sins.

Yom Kippur is the most solemn day of the Jewish year.

Starting at sundown on Yom Kippur Eve, devout Jews fast for twenty-four hours. (All Jewish holidays begin at sunset the evening before and last until the next sunset.) They go to pray in the temple that evening and the next day. At sundown a long loud sound is blown on the shofar. It is the signal that the Book of Life is closed, and a new year is beginning.

58

Succoth, or the Festival of the Booths, is a week of thanksgiving for the harvest and comes five days after the Day of Atonement. Many families who have yards or gardens build little outdoor booths in memory of the time during the Flight from Egypt when the Jews lived in such shelters. The booths are decorated with squashes and pumpkins, ripe corn and grapes, apples and nuts. For a week the family eats its meals in the booth.

Hanukah is the Festival of Lights, the holiday that Jewish children love most. It comes in midwinter, usually in December. Hanukah is the season of gift giving and parties.

This holiday is observed in memory of the time over 2,100 years ago when a brave Jew named Judah Maccabaeus got back the great Temple at Jerusalem which had been taken over by the Syrians. One day's supply of holy oil — all that was left — burned miraculously in the temple lamp for eight days, until new oil could be prepared and blessed. Because the oil lasted so long it was called a miracle.

To celebrate this holiday Jews light an eight-branched candlestick called a Menorah. One candle is lit the first night, then one more each night until all eight are lit. The children play with a top with four sides bearing the Hebrew letters N G H S. They stand for the Hebrew words which mean "a great miracle happened there" — the miracle of the temple oil.

Purim is a spring holiday held in March in honor of the time long ago in the land of Persia when good Queen Esther and her cousin Mordecai saved the Jews from being killed by wicked Haman's plot. In the synagogue children shake a rattle and shout fiercely when Haman's name is said as the Bible story is told. At this time families have fancy dress parties and special cakes are eaten.

Passover, a great holiday which celebrates the Jews' escape from Egypt in the time of Moses, usually comes in April. It begins with a festive supper called the Seder. Passover lasts a week, during which time only unleavened bread called matzoth — bread made without yeast — may be eaten. In the Flight from Egypt the Jews had no time to let their bread rise, and this custom recalls that haste.

At the traditional Seder, symbolic foods are put on the table to remind the Jews of their misery in the land of Egypt and their joy when Moses led them to the Promised Land. The youngest son of the family askes four questions about the meaning of the Seder, and the father answers him. After the story of the Seder supper has been told, the family eats a festive meal.

Passover has been celebrated continuously since Biblical times. It is one of the oldest festivals of freedom in the world.

BOOKS TO READ ABOUT HOLIDAYS

The Christmas Book of Legends and Stories, compiled by Elva
Smith and Alice Hazeltine. Lothrop, Lee and Shepard Co.,
Inc.
A wide variety of stories about Christmas taken from Bib-
lical, folk, and present-day sources.

The Easter Book of Legends and Stories, compiled by Alice
Hazeltine. Lothrop, Lee and Shepard Co., Inc.
Many stories of Easter and the renewal of life in the spring-
time from various sources.

Halloween through Twenty Centuries, by Ralph and Adeline
Linton. Abelard-Schuman, Inc.
Tracing the holiday down through the ages, this book tells
the religious and magical folklore that has grown up
around it.

INDEX

HOLIDAYS · HOLIDAYS